THE WAY IT WAS

Zella Mangold Lockard

Illustrations by the Author

First Edition
Library of Congress Catalog Card Number 86-61260
ISBN 0-914468-10-3

Published by PEPPER PUBLISHING
2901 East Mabel Street
Tucson, AZ 85716

PRINTED IN THE UNITED STATES OF AMERICA

TABLE OF CONTENTS

THE SETTING

I was born in a farm home, built by my Great-Grandfather Lamer, 2 1/2 miles north of Cobden, Illinois on a cold, snowy February day in 1905. Cobden is located in the middle of Union County, Illinois in the hill country. The western boundary of our county is the Mississippi River, and about one third of the county is near the river. That land (near the river), is low and flat and more fertile than the hills in the other section. For the most part, it was farmed in large tracts by tenant farmers. The people who owned the farms lived in the towns nearby.

Our part of the county is very hilly and the farms were smaller and partially wooded. A 100-acre farm was considered "large." We lived in the foothills of the Ozark Range, which starts in Missouri and continues across southern Illinois into Indiana. Bald Knob, the highest "hill" in Union County, can be seen for miles around and is the second highest spot in the state. The farms were divided into parts. The highest ridges were planted in fruit trees; some of the lower, more level ground grew vegetables and small fruits; and the lowest meadows were left in grasses, and the hay was cut, dried and hauled to the barns to feed livestock.

We lived in the Lamer community, as four of the neighboring farms were owned by Lamer families. My father and mother purchased the 72-acre farm from Great-Grandmother Lamer, after her husband's death. Dad worked and managed the farm and paid for it, also providing a home for great-grandmother. Some of our neighbors inherited their farms and had something with which to start, so they did not have to be as frugal as we did, to make a "go of it."

There was no motorized farm equipment. All the plowing and cultivating was done by horse and mule-pulled plows and harrows. In 1920 this was still true. Every farm had to have a barn to house the horses, mules and cows and to store hay and corn to feed them.

We had no electricity and had to rely on kerosene lamps. Some people in Cobden had gas lights, but very few. We did have a Hay Seed telephone line (its real name), with one operator at the switchboard in the village of Cobden. To call the operator, or any other person on the line, you had to "turn a crank." Everyone on the line had a combination of long and short rings. I believe there were thirteen parties on the line and a lot of conversation took place across the miles. You always had to be sure there was no conversation going on, on the line, before you tried to ring "Central," the switchboard operator. If you didn't make sure the line was clear, and rang the phone in somebody's ear, it was bad. There were some who abused the privilege of having a telephone and monopolized the line at times.

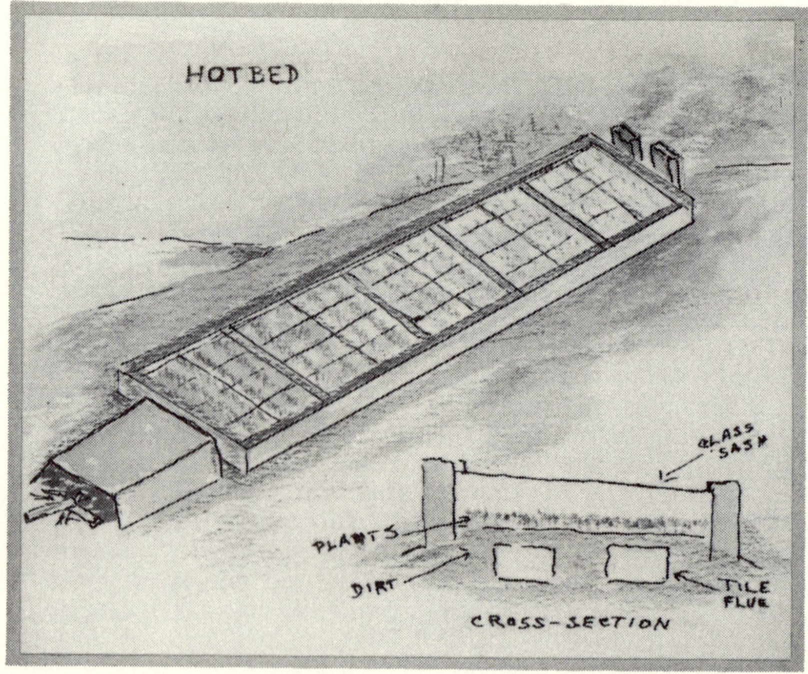

THE SEASONS
BEGINNING WITH SPRING

I have chosen to divide my descriptions of various farm and home activities into the categories of the four seasons. The seasons in our part of the country are distinctly different and daily activities changed as the seasons did. I will begin with the spring season because it was (and still is) my favorite. Spring was the season of transition from the severe winters to the wonderful sunny, summer days of June, July and August. Everything that occurred pointed to a new life, a new beginning, another chance.

SPRING IN ALL ITS GLORY

Since the southern part of Illinois is as far south as Richmond, Virginia, our weather was seldom extreme and then only for short periods of time. Every few years we might have an extra cold winter (with temperatures below zero), or a very dry, hot summer (sometimes with near 100-degree temperatures), or a spring with too many inches of rainfall, but most of the time the weather followed a sensible pattern.

When we began to tire of the drabness of winter, the bareness of the trees, the brown grass, the freezing and thawing and the mud, and the lack of something growing, we got narcissus bulbs and put them in containers with rocks and water and kept them in a dark place until they rooted. Then we brought them up from the cellar into the light and enjoyed their fragrant blossoms for several weeks. Many people had amaryllis bulbs set away, growing in tubs or large pots, and later they were beautiful and showy when they bloomed in a sunny window.

On most farms, there were little wisps of smoke rising from wooden flues of hot beds, where tomato, pepper and sweet potato plants were being started to plant in the fields. These little plants were cared for routinely, not allowed to get too dry, and were watered or the glass sash pulled back, to get the benefit of a warm spring shower. The slow-burning fires had to be kept burning and sometimes, on cold nights, trips had to be made in the middle of the night to keep the fire burning and the seedlings warm.

We had two tenant houses on the farm to house families for farm labor, with rent free. The farm had to be managed so the laborers could be assured of regular pay checks for their work, to buy staple groceries for their families. Some of the tenant laborers lived with us for five to ten years. Every farmer had his own cow to furnish milk and butter and cheese for the family. In my childhood there were no dairies. My father furnished feed and pasture for a cow of each tenant. Every tenant had a vegetable garden and a flock of chickens for eggs and meat for the table.

We had a neighbor family who lived a short distance from us with whom we had a close relationship: Uncle Witt and Aunt Laura Lamer and their five children. Other neighbors had farms with homes from 1/2 to 1 mile apart. Their homes and buildings were placed on the highest ground of the farm acreage.

I remember seeing my father and Uncle Witt Lamer meet down the road, halfway between our houses, to compare work that was going on currently on their two farms. They tried to decide the proper time to start application of a certain spray for the fruit or when to start pruning or picking. After a heavy freeze in the early spring, they brought sample branches from the trees, let them warm up in the house, then they cut the buds open to see how many had survived. They could tell immediately. It was a sad day when they discovered that most of the fruit had been killed out for the coming harvest season. Those two men were very close friends and were of much help to each other.

One of the earliest events that I can REALLY remember was when little Grandmother Lamer passed away. Everything was strange. I suppose my little girl routine was upset. Unusual things happened around the house: whispered conversations, closed doors, strange people coming and going. My Great-Aunt Nora came from Portland, Oregon. She was grandma's daughter who lived far, far away. She brought my brother and me some pretty felt houseslippers, which is probably why I remember her. I corresponded with her in later years but never saw her again. The house reeked with floral scents, particularly of carnations. To this day, the spicy smell of carnations makes me think of funerals. My

10

parents left me at the farm home with strange relatives when they left for the burial service in Cobden, but I still remember watching that procession of horse-drawn vehicles, the hearse in particular, leaving the house that cold winter day.

Every farm had a martin box, and early in March this box, which looked like a "doll apartment house" on top of a big high pole, was made ready for the purple, iridescent colored, migratory birds that came back and forth from South America, arriving every year on March 18 and leaving for their long trip back south on August 18. These were very noisy, active birds. Sometimes the sky would be full of them, for they fed on flying insects. They helped to reduce the mosquito population around a farm. They also fought off the chicken hawks, which preyed on mother hens and their baby chicks. The martins liked to live in colonies (hence the apartment house), and one box would house many families. They also would tolerate a few sparrows who would "mooch" a space or two and live with them. They were not song birds, but had a very unpleasant (but friendly) sound they made when they were congregating. We were always aware that they were around.

Dogwood trees bloomed in the edges of the woods, in under the larger forest trees. The dogwood tree is beautiful and grows and blooms anywhere it can have fifty-percent shade. Redbud trees also bloom when the dogwood does and they grow under the same set of circumstances. Rows of lilac bushes were blooming early in spring in most farmyards.

Because the bright blooms of wild flowers attracted my attention, I became interested in things of nature and tried to learn the names of all growing things. Our region of Illinois is a perfect place for nature study. We have been told, because of the movement of the glaciers in our area, that we have the largest assortment of growing plants on the North American continent.

Another early harbinger of spring was the sarvis berry bush; which grew in the woods and was the first tree that bloomed in the spring, with a feathery, white spray. About the same time one could take note of the ruby red, swollen buds of the soft maples and the buds of the pussy willow trees. On the grassy slopes, we looked

for the small "bluets," which looked like tiny blue blossoms embroidered on the grassy rug. On wooded slopes, spring beauties, another delicate flower, could always be found the first few sunny days we had in the spring. In areas around the houses, crocuses and yellow blossoms of jonquils, with their dark green leaves, became to come up through the grass. We always had clumps of sweet-smelling English violets on the south side of our house and if you kept the blossoms picked, they continued to bloom for a long time. The fruit orchards, which bloomed a little later (apples, peaches, plums, pears and cherries), were always beautiful when the buds had not been winter killed, and they colored the landscape with their pastel blocks of blossoms.

I knew where the Virginia blue bells were to be found along the banks of streams, also sweet williams and yellow, white and blue violets. These were all growing wild and they came up year after year. On the high, rocky places, where the big rocks were exposed, there were banks of shooting stars. Mayapples spread their green umbrellas and bloomed in the fence corners. On one special rock in a neighbor's pasture, we found a Dutchman's breeches plant. The plant has leaves like a miniature bleeding heart, but the blossoms are white and do look like a little pair of pants. I know that after seventy years have come and gone, if I could get to that place on the rock, I'd find the same wild flowers there.

12

Later the wild roses bloomed in fence rows and in uncultivated parts of farms. Wild blackberries and dewberries bloomed and if undisturbed, bore luscious berries for the picking. They made delicious jellies and jams.

Along with all these delectable goodies from Mother Nature came some undesirable things to beware of. Before taking a stroll out in the rough part of farms, you had to understand that all things out there were not as desirable as those we have been talking about. First, everywhere you went there were poison ivy plants, those three-leaved vines that must be avoided with a passion. Then there was that pesky parasitic larvae which Webster calls the "chigger." This little pest can bury itself under your skin, at the tops of your socks, at your waistband, in your armpits, etc. It's best to be prepared against this small pest, by rubbing your ankles and legs with powdered sulphur before going out to admire Mother Nature in the rough.

Anyone who grew up on a farm will never forget the smell of the earth as it was turned over by the plow, for making the vegetable garden ready to plant. That is a "spring smell." We didn't have much to do with planting on the big farm acreage, but we did help with our little family garden. Helping to prepare the Irish potatoes for planting in the trench was fun. The potatoes had to be cut into pieces, so that each piece had an eye to produce a sprout for a plant in the row. They had to be spaced equal distances apart. I also got to help drop the English peas in the trench. It was quite an accomplishment to get your garden planted before your neighbor got his in the ground.

Pretty soon it was time to begin cutting the asparagus stalks for packing and shipping. This is the time that the young folks and children were brought into the farming operation. We had to work right along with the children of the tenant farmer, in the asparagus field. We had a long asparagus knife with a forked notch on the cutting blade. We had to walk down the long rows, lean over and cut the stalk well below the level of the ground, to be picked up in a basket later. Then it was taken to the shed and bunched and packed. I never did like this work, for it was a backbreaking job. The asparagus harvest lasted about six weeks, and it was a glorious day when Dad said he was going to "lay the asparagus by." That meant we would stop cutting and shipping and let the beds rest. Usually dirt was thrown up over the rows with a plow. The asparagus grew up through the soil which covered it, went to seed, and looked like a huge bed of asparagus fern. But it would be ready for cutting the following spring.

14

SUMMERTIME

After the cold winter was almost gone, we had the blustery, stormy month of March to endure, which could be winter and could also be spring. This was the month when the threat of cyclones hovered over us much of the time. Before I was born, we had a cyclone which blew away the barn on the farm and completely demolished one of the tenant houses. After that experience, our parents were very conscious of dark, ominous skies that might develop at any time into a funnel cloud. I can remember, as a little girl, being awakened in the middle of the night and going down to the cellar (our only safe place), with a kerosene light or lantern. Periodically (while we were down there), our parents would climb the steps to look out at the sky in order to determine our immediate danger. Such storms were frightening, with dark, dark clouds and thunder and flashes of lightning. But I do not remember a storm doing any damage while I lived on the farm. We were just apprehensive. Some people did not have a cellar under their house and they dug and built a small storm cellar close to the house, to go to for safety, should their house lie in the path of the storm.

When March was over and done with, we had the month of April with its spring rains, before vacation time came. In those days, we had only an eight-month school term. The last day of school was quite a special day, usually with a picnic. Prizes were given out to those who had earned them. Seldom did we have regular classes.

But for even those who professed to like school, it was a welcome day. It was a sort of change of pace and activity different than what we had to follow all winter. One always had to have something new to wear in celebration of the day.

Summer was a busy, bustling time of the year. Our farm was mainly a fruit farm, with apples and peaches and pears on the ridges of ground that, by elevation, were more protected from the sub-zero killing winter temperature. My father raised asparagus and rhubarb also. The fruit trees had to be sprayed at regular times during the year. They had to be pruned in the early winter. I was never involved in any of this activity.

In the summer there was much activity that went on around the house. We had a live-in hired girl or one who came in for the day. I became her chief helper. Mom was in the packing shed most of the day, so I learned to do many household tasks early in life. Cooking the meals for a hungry bunch of farm workers each day was a big job. We always fed from eight to ten people each day.

It was an established fact that Saturday evening, sometimes before and sometimes after supper, we had a gallon and a half of homemade ice cream (cooked with eggs and lots of good milk and cream). Someone coming from town brought an extra big chunk of ice and mom had the custard cooked and cooling. Sometimes I had to sit on top of the freezer on a pillow to hold it down during the last stages of the freezing. When they took out the dasher, I got to get some pretasting (we called it licking-the-paddle). Then the freezer was repacked and set aside to get more solid and season. Then everybody had all they could eat.

Sometimes between crops and always at the end of the fruit harvest, we had a Sunday safari (usually no more than 35 miles) to a picnic site and had a lunch. There were many interruptions along the way. The roads we travelled were dirt and gravel. Flat tires were very common. Spark plugs had to be cleaned. Sometimes work had to be done on something called a "magneto." Sometimes the cars got hot and wouldn't run, started steaming, and we had to get a bucket of water for the radiator from the creek or the nearest farm house.

Many farmer's wives had beautiful summer flower gardens, but my mother was too busy helping with the farm chores and keeping the house going to have much time for real flower gardening. But there was a wealth of beauty all around. Day lilies were in all the fence corners, wild daisies, Queen Anna's lace, black-eyed-susans, honeysuckle, milkweed, wild asters—every telephone pole had a trumpet vine.

AUTUMN

When the last of the peaches had been picked from the trees in August, we began to think about the first day of school in September. Although we liked school, we never were quite ready to give up the free days of summer for the confinement of classes, books and learning.

Fall apples (Jonathan, Winesap, etc.), were part of the farm crops; they were always processed after school had started. Our parents thought our place was in school when school was in session. We were never kept out of school to help harvest apples. Many farmers grew sweet potatoes and this was the time for digging them. Many of the one-room rural schools dismissed so the children could help with the sweet potatoes.

A TIME OF BEAUTY

As a child (my mother being an artist), I was always trying to draw and color country scenes with the beautiful colors of fall, after a frosty period of weather. I remember drawing a hillside with a row of sassafras bushes along a barbed wire fence, with a beautiful blue sky and green hillside. It made a pretty picture and I drew many variations of this scene. There were ruby red sumac bushes along a rail fence or on a distant ridge. Goldenrod was blooming all over the countryside, as were the lavender-colored wild asters and purple clustered blossoms of ironweed. We had a yard full of hard maples, and they were nearly always a beautiful clear yellow. I always was fascinated by the neat, shiny, dark red leaves of the black gum. You would find these leaves on the ground in the woods and have to look way, way up to see the tops of the tree. It was the sweet gum trees that were like Joseph's "coat of many colors." They were yellow, orange, red, brown, green and almost black (such a dark red), all on one tree. The dogwood trees that had been covered with white blossoms in the spring turned a beautiful rosy red, with clusters of bright red berries.

MAKING APPLE BUTTER (AUTUMN ACTIVITY)

This was a very specialized kind of undertaking. A day prior to the cooking of the apple butter, neighbors would come to help peel and prepare the apples. Sometimes three or four families would make it a joint effort. The apples were cooked outside in a big copper kettle, or wash boiler, and a wood fire kept going under the kettle. Some people added apple cider to give the butter a more tart taste. It was given a spicy flavor by using some form of cinnamon (powdered or pieces of the cinnamon bark tied in a cloth); others used red-hot cinnamon candies. Of course, after the apples were cooked down considerably, sugar was added to make it palatable. None of the above activity could have taken place without the help of the apple butter paddle. Usually every household had one handed down through generations. It had no other use but to stir the bubbling, boiling mass in the kettle. The paddle had a 5-foot handle attached to a wooden paddle 20 inches long and 8 inches wide. This paddle was bored full of holes an inch in diameter. The holes allowed the apple butter to flow through while the paddle was stirring. Someone always had to "man" the paddle, for you couldn't afford to let the apple butter burn or stick to the bottom of the kettle. There was always the tasting and the testing for consistency. It had to be cooked, until when cooled it would spread without running off your piece of buttered bread. It surely tasted good with country sausage and hot biscuits.

Fall was also a time for nut gathering. Our pasture had about a dozen large scaly-bark hickory nut trees. All other trees were cut down when the ground was cleared of forest. Most of the land on our farm, at one time, had been covered with native forest. I can remember dad referring to some acreage at the back of the farm as being "new ground." He meant that it was newly cleared, trees cut, and stumps grubbed and burned out, and ready for cultivation. Some pretty fall Sunday, our family invited relatives and friends to come out and have potluck (everybody bring a dish) and we gathered the hickory nuts out of the pasture. The men would climb the trees or use a log to bump the tree trunk and shake

them, then we all picked them up and hulled. We left some for the squirrels. There were many black walnuts too, but for some reason our farm did not have any walnut trees.

Most farmers raised their own pork. The pigs were fed well and fattened all summer, then one cold winter day they were butchered and the pork meat processed. Some was salted down to be smoked at a later time. Some was ground and made into sausage and canned (a process of frying it and covering it with lard and sealing it). Some people made link sausage. Head cheese was one of the tastier items that came from the leftover parts that were edible, mainly from the head of the pig. The heart and liver of the animal were also used for food. All this took place before the time we had frozen lockers and commercial meat processing. It was a sort of do-it-yourself, with your neighbors' help; and you helped him in return.

The days kept getting shorter and the nights a little cooler. Finally, one day we could look up and the pretty colored leaves had all come down and we had only bare limbs and scattered green cedars on the hillsides. Winter was gradually edging out autumn with its icy fingers. Then we had a light snow and we knew it was time for growing things to take a rest.

WINTER

Wintertime was the part of the year that activities in our climate were curtailed because of weather conditions: growing things were dormant; the trees were bare of leaves; and everything was dull and lifeless. It was a time for spending more time indoors. Anything that could be kept for winter use had been canned and stored. I can remember that certain people had buildings they used, and rented to others, for the storage of sweet potatoes. That was one crop that was held and sold at a later date. The potatoes had to be kept dry, to keep from rotting, and warm enough not to freeze. Many farmers stored their apples, potatoes, turnips and sometimes cabbage, for family use, in large dug out storage holes in the ground, insulated with dirt and straw. If this was done correctly, the produce, which was put in, came out with a nice crisp taste and was never frozen. Yes, winter was a time for enjoying those things we had prepared all summer to use in the cold time ahead.

We had no natural lakes in the community where we lived. Farm ponds were made in strategic spots by building dirt dams. These ponds provided water for the livestock and for spraying the fruit trees. Sometimes, in wintertime, the temperature was cold enough, and stayed that way long enough, to freeze the water in the ponds with ice thick enough to skate on. We were always anxious to strap on our skates, but were never allowed on the ice until our dad had tested it to see if it was thick enough to be safe for us. When conditions were right, we organized skating parties, built bonfires to get warm by on the pond dams and tried to enjoy this exhilarating activity. I never learned to skate very well. The ice always melted before I had enough practice, and my ankles were very weak, allowing my feet to flop over to one side or the other.

When we had several inches of snow, we began to look for our sleds, and several families had homemade bobsleds that four or five could pile on. That was a lot of fun, and the topography of our part of the country is such that the slopes were perfect for bobsled runs. I always felt sorry for kids that lived in flat country, with no downhill slopes. Sometimes we had thick sleet on top of snow and we scooted down the straight slopes on strips of corrugated tin. One family in our community had a hill slope that was "super" for sledding, and they helped us to keep snow on the bare spots so we could enjoy the run down the hill, after the snow began to melt in spots on the hillside.

Bowls of big, juicy, red apples and big pans of popcorn are also in my medley of winter memories. Sometimes we had taffy pulls and at times mom would make a batch of taffy with hickory nuts. Nothing else in the world like it!! Some folks had some peanuts growing along with the sweet potatoes and these were good roasted in a wood stove oven.

We had many forecasters who claimed they could predict the severity of winter's cold blasts by observing some of nature's signs, such as the color of the coverings of wooly worms, the thickness of the husks on the corn, the heavy or light fur coats on the fur-bearing animals. But no one could predict the weather every time. Old Man Winter seemed to always come unannounced and left just as stealthily.

During the winter months, I missed the flowers of the other seasons. It was so good to see the crocuses peeping through the snow. Many years I have seen jonquils all budded out, just ready to bloom, almost covered with snow. If a person wanted flowers in winter, plants like amaryllis and Christmas cactus had to be grown in large containers. I have seen small washtubs just filled with gorgeous amaryllis blooms at some farmer's wife's window in the dead of winter. Everybody always got a thrill from a Christmas cactus which bloomed when it was supposed to bloom.

SCHOOL

We lived in the northeast corner of the Cobden School District #17. Originally, our farm was in the Limestone one-room country school district. Although we lived in the Lamer community, and there was a Lamer one-room school also, our parents wanted us to attend the village of Cobden public school where all the grades were separated, so they made the necessary arrangements for this to be possible, and we were transferred from one district to the other.

My first and only school house was a two-story brick building in the village of Cobden where my mother and my grandmother went to school. We lived over two miles in the country and we walked most every day. Of course, there were older children to look after me as a beginner (I started to school when I was 5), but at any time, it was a long trek. In the winter, it was almost dark when we finished the long walk home. On rainy, or stormy, snowy days, our parents provided some kind of horse-drawn conveyance to come and get us. We rarely had to walk in the rain. We wore high button shoes and rubbers or overshoes (the buckle kind) in the rain and snow. Our feet were muddy most of the time.

There were two routes that we could take to school, you might say the high path and the low road. The low road was the public one travelled by the people who lived out our way. If we chose that one, a friendly farmer might come along and give us a lift. In the 2-mile stretch of road to town, there were six or seven bridges across a winding stream. The high path was just a "way to go," or a footpath through folk's backyards, across ploughed fields and fences, across one footbridge, up to the top of the wooded ridge and back down again. In the wintertime, the ground that was frozen and easy to walk over in the morning could be very muddy and sticky by midafternoon. We were never dismissed until four o'clock. The high route to school ended up on top of a rocky outcropping overlooking the school and the play yard full of children. When we got to that point in the morning it was a relief, for it was all downhill from there on. It was a good feeling to reach that point about 8:30 a.m. and we were seldom late. It broke my heart to be tardy. I must have developed the habit of being on time early in my young life. I always planned to start in time.

We were very fortunate in our Cobden schools to have an excellent school and teachers who were dedicated, professional people. I particularly remember two of them: Pearl McDaniel, my 5th grade teacher, and Mamie Clutts, my 8th grade teacher, who was also my freshman English teacher. Both of these teachers were TOPS.

My closest friend through the twelve (really eleven for I passed over the first) years of schooling was Mildred Anderson, who lived on a farm about a mile south of our home. Her mother and mine were also school pals. Mildred and I always had the best grades in our class, yet there was no cutthroat competition. When we graduated, my marks for the four high school years were slightly better than hers. I was valedictorian of our class and she was salutatorian. There was no resentment on her part.

Our school board worked very hard all the time, year after year, to improve our public schools. For years our high school wasn't accredited by state authorities. But this was accomplished a year or two before I graduated in 1922. My father served one term on the school board, but he soon decided that there were too many meetings and too many problems to be resolved, and it was too time-consuming for him, so he bowed out.

INTERESTING SPOTS ON THE LOW ROAD

On the side of the road about halfway to the school in Cobden, there lived a family (mother and daughter) who operated a loom and did a lot of weaving of rag rugs. Every 1st or 2nd grade class in Cobden grade school had a field trip out to Mrs. Click's home. She and her daughter, Matilda, did their weaving in a small building next to her home. She explained the entire process to us and it was quite enlightening. Later I helped my mother tear strips of rags from discarded, worn-out clothing and sew the strips together. Then we rolled them in big balls and stored them in big cloth sacks. Periodically, when we had accumulated enough rags (by pounds), or enough balls (by count), we took them to Mrs. Click and she furnished the warp and charged us by the yard for weaving them into throw rugs.

A little further down the road was the blacksmith shop of Mr. Frank Rose. The road passed real close to the shop and oftentimes we saw the red coals of the fire and the red hot metal he was pounding on the anvil, shaping for some purpose or another. At other times, he was bent over, with a horse's foot between his knees, nailing a shoe on a horse. Spans of horses and mules were often tied outside the shop, waiting for him to get the shoes prepared. This was a fascinating place, but we never stopped, because we were told not to disturb him as he worked. So we observed what he was doing and passed on by.

Just a little further toward town and very near the Whelpley house, where we left the public highway and walked across farmland, was a grove of trees and a little hill on the road that was called "Slaughter Pen Hill." It was here that the butchers brought the cattle to butcher them for sale at the local meat counters in the stores. There was a pen back from the road, almost out of sight, where the cattle were unloaded. We never saw any of the butchery, but we knew what went on.

In the same grove of trees, nearer the road, there was a spot where groups of wandering gypsies stopped to camp. I can remember their gaudy, painted wagons where they lived and the strings of wares they were selling; also the full-skirted, brightly dressed women and their campfires. When we passed their camp, it was always daylight and they meant us no harm, but they had a quality about them of the unknown, unfamiliar way of life and that was frightening to us as children.

THE ORDEAL OF LONG UNDERWEAR

In the early years of the twentieth century most houses were not heated uniformly. The fireplaces, heating and cooking stoves were all wood burning, and had to be stoked frequently. We were exposed to winter's cold blasts in our long treks to and from school and we had to wear warmer clothing than today. So we had to wear what we called long-legged or "long-handled" underwear.

The underwear, for the most part, was made of cotton knit and it stretched easily. Nobody, child or adult, liked to wear the hated garment but it was necessary for warmth. It was worn next to the skin and one had to stretch the lower part of the leg of the underwear to get it on over the foot, so it wasn't exactly form-fitting around the ankle. We wore knee-length cotton stockings and it was a trick to get the excess underwear (which had been stretched over the foot), neatly wrapped around the ankle and lower leg and covered smoothly with the stocking. There were always lumps and bulges, although men and women could hide these with their long skirts and long pants. On the second day of wear, the underwear was somewhat stretched all over, and by the middle of the week you didn't feel comfortable in it; it felt baggy and IT WAS BAGGY.

It was a great day when mom decided it was safe (fearing the exposure would give us pneumonia) to discard the long-handles for lighter, more comfortable garments. Sometimes winter came back and we had to submit again to the indignities of the long underwear to keep our bodies warm, but it usually was for a very short period.

Then a day of more body freedom came, early in the summer after school was over for the year. This usually happened sometime in mid-May and was the day we could discard our shoes and stockings and go barefoot at home. How good and cool that green grass felt to our hot feet. Our bare feet got various injuries, stubbed toes, numerous cuts and bee stings from the white clover in the grass. When we had to dress up to go out and it came time to put shoes on our liberated feet, there was a lot of moaning and groaning and limping. Sometimes we had to stay home. The shoes were too painful to endure.

CLOTHING

Most of our clothing was homemade. About the only thing we ordered from the catalog or bought at the store was underwear and heavy coats. Sometimes we had a woolen dress or two. The summer dresses were gingham, percale, voile and organdy (all cotton, no synthetics). The more affluent had silk and satin and blouses of crepe-de-chine. Even when I was a BIG girl, my mother wouldn't let me wear silk. She associated fine clothes with proud, haughty people and she didn't want me to become like them.

Our first shoes were button shoes and a button hook was necessary to get them fastened. Later we had shoes that laced. When I was in the 6th grade we had an out-of-town teacher who was a high-stepper, or so we thought. She wore two-toned, high heeled shoes that laced over the calves of her legs.

For muddy roads we had rubbers or overshoes that came up to the ankles and buckled. Both men and women wore these. Galoshes were unheard of. If you had to get out in deep mud, you wore gum boots that came to your knees.

Women at work outside in the yard or garden, during the summer months, wore bonnets with "tails" to cover their necks and keep them from getting freckled or sunburned. They were similar to the bonnets worn by the Amish women today. I never did like to wear a bonnet, although my mother was after me constantly to put one on. If some women were going to be out in the sun for long periods, they put stocking legs on their arms to keep from getting sunburned. That is a far cry from today's woman, who goes outside (anywhere) with "short shorts" and a bandeau. Things have changed.

MONDAY MORNING - THE LAUNDRY ROUTINE

One of the most transformed household chores in a family's routine, in my lifetime, is that of washday or the weekly laundry. For some reason this day always had to be on Monday. Even though it looked like rain, the process was started. Nothing short of a downpour or a blizzard would stop the preliminary preparations.

On the farm, we usually had one of the tenant's wives help with the heavy work, like carrying water and big baskets of wet clothes to the clothesline on the other side of the house. Sometimes the kettle for heating water was some distance from the well.

Most every farm home had a rain barrel where soft rain water was collected for laundry purposes as it ran off the roof of a building. We had a big, iron kettle where water was heated to start the washer going with warm water. This was before we had awareness of "acid rain," and we thought rain water was the purest, softest water to have.

The dirty clothes were collected and sorted in piles to be washed together. I can remember playing in the piles of soiled clothes and getting them all messed up, with resulting reprimands. But as I remember it, we had a lot of fun with lace curtains and mom's long skirts.

Sheets and tablecloths were washed first, and everything white had to be boiled in the iron kettle (with a little lye in the water for bleaching purposes). Then these white clothes, in fact all the clothes, had to be "squished" through two rinses and run through the wringer. White shirts had to be starched with cooked starch. We used ARGO, but some people used flour for starch.

Folks who didn't own a wooden-tubbed washer, with a dolly propelled by a cogwheel (which was turned back and forth by a hand lever), had to rub the clothes on a washboard in a tin tub (a back- breaking job). As I grew older, I had to push the lever on the washer back and forth a lot of the time, as well as turn the crank for the wringer.

It was a half-day's work to do the family wash, provided the weather cooperated. Sometimes you took the clothes down for a shower and pinned them back on the line several times during the day. My mother was very particular about how the clothes were pinned to the line. She thought they were easier to iron if they were straight and the wrinkles were blown out by the breeze. Sometimes the wind almost blew them into the next forty. Mom was also very particular about hanging underwear and the ragged part of the wash in the back, where passersby could not see them. Then late Monday we took the dry clothes off the line and dampened them for ironing on Tuesday. Mondays and Tuesdays were ususally spent after this pattern. If something happened and the washing and ironing did not get finished on Tuesday, the rest of the week was all fouled-up. Tuesday, a big fire was built in the wood-burning kitchen stove to heat the flat irons and another half day was spent in ironing the dampened clothes. My father's collars and cuffs had to be cold starched and ironed dry. This was quite a chore for a little girl to learn, but I finally did. In 1923, when I was 17 years old, I took over the running of our farm household because of my mother's ill health. But when it came to ironing, I thought I would never become good enough at it to be trusted with more than the bandanna handkerchiefs.

Just in passing, I will add that in our household that Tuesday also became a day to bake the light bread and rolls for a several day supply, because we had the stove going and the oven was hot. At any rate, it was the day we did all kinds of cooking in the oven.

Of course, the coming of electricity revolutionized all this. A housewife can wash and dry her dirty clothes anytime, night or day. Nobody boils clothes now, ready-made solutions take care of that.

FRUIT FARMING

Horticulture, the raising of fruit trees, peaches, apples and pears, was brought to our part of the county by families from New England. The topography of our area of the county was similar to their farmland in the East and they brought their "know how" with them. Since our soil was basically yellow clay, they had to blast holes in the soil to plant the young trees, which were spaced at regular intervals in the orchard. Peach orchards, as a rule, were cultivated, but I remember the apple and pear orchards as having a cover of grass on the ground.

The trees had to be sprayed for various diseases of the tree itself, and to protect the young fruit from damaging insects which deposited their eggs in the green fruit; the larvae then infested the ripening fruit and spoiled it for shipping. A wormy apple or peach does not mature properly and will not carry to market. They end up in the cull box and have to be thrown away.

Besides all this care of spraying, the trees had to be pruned each fall or winter to shape the trees, get rid of the dead growth and provide a maximum number of buds for the next year's crop.

Even back in the days of my childhood, the care of a fruit orchard was a scientific venture and everything had to be done at the proper time. You just can't plant trees and forget them and expect a good crop of fruit each year. I have known city people who come to small towns and immediately plant every kind of fruit tree they see in the nursery catalogs. They do not know what they are getting into and are not prepared to scientifically care for the trees. In a short time they become disillusioned and disappointed and the trees have to be removed. They find out the hard way.

Harvest time in the fruit orchard always had to begin before the fruit was completely ripe. The first picking got the largest and ripest fruit, but it was always a little premature. Usually the trees had to be picked over two, three or maybe four times. In the early days, the pickers used one-half bushel baskets and ladders, pouring the fruit into bushel boxes to be hauled to the packing shed on a flat-bedded, low wagon. Much fruit was bruised and mashed with all the handling. Today they use cloth picking bags and many dwarf variety trees can be picked without the use of ladders.

We used to sort every peach or apple by hand as to size, imperfection, etc. There were usually two grades, #1 and #2. The smaller size was #2 and, of course, all the rest went into the cull box, below the packing bench. We had to shake down each basket of fruit and, by hand, put the rings of fruit around the top of the basket before the lid was put on. Today, the large fruit growers have graders, which wash the fruit before it passes over rollers spaced to allow the small fruit to fall through cracks and be transmitted to another roller. The more perfect and larger fruit continues on the moving belt to be packed as #1, or the cream of the crop. People still have to be hired to stand on each side of the grader to pick out the faulty, or rottenspotted fruit from the grader as the fruit rolls by, but they don't have to worry about undersize fruit, the grader has done that.

WINTER BUSINESS ON THE FARM

Somewhere in this book I mentioned the fact that farmers had to manage the farm work so the tenant workers had some work to do the year-round.

Since my father raised fruit trees, the orchard trees had to be pruned every winter, usually in late fall before the buds for blooming the next year were too far advanced. This was a scientific process, for the older growth had to be cut and the trees shaped so the fruit would develop uniformly all over the tree and could be reached with ladders at picking time. Then the trees had to be hand sprayed, using a wooden tank to hold the liquid on a wagon with a gasoline pump for pressure for the spray. The spray wagons were pulled through the orchards by teams of horses and mules. I can remember the chug-chugging of the pumps and the smell of the lime and sulphur mixture that was used to wet the trees in an effort to control the San Jose scale (a disease of the bark of the peach and apple trees). This had to be applied when the trees were bare.

Then the trees and other growing farm produce had to be fertilized and there were no commercial fertilizers in those days. We had some stable manure from the barn animals, but much more was needed. So carloads of stable manure were ordered through the local People's Fruit and Vegetable Shippers Ass'n. (a forerunner of the co-ops), from the National Stockyards at East St. Louis or the stockyards in Chicago. These malodorous carloads of freight were switched off the trains at Cobden and transferred by each farmer to his farm. The whole countryside reeked when farmers sent their teams and wagons with sideboards, and a man or two on each wagon with a pitch fork to transfer the manure, forkful by forkful, from the boxcars, to the wagon, to the farm. The manure was put around each fruit tree, on the rows of asparagus and on the hills of rhubarb.

I remember seeing the hired men digging the dirt away from the base of the trunks of peach and apple trees in order to expose the wood and dig out the borer with knives. Then the dirt had to be put back. It was painstaking work. Later a chemical was developed, "para-dichlorobenzine," which was referred to as PDB (which

smelled like moth balls) and this was used to scatter around the base of the tree. It was very potent, but it did away with those tedious, costly hours of work digging the borers out. It had to be carefully stored, for it was very penetrating. If it was placed anywhere that your chickens could get to it, even the eggs they laid tasted of the chemical and were unfit for use.

When the men began to catch up on all the wintertime chores on the farm, and there wasn't much left to do, dad put them to work cutting down trees in the woods, and sawing the wood for our stoves and for theirs, also. There was quite an acreage of woods at the north end of the farm and plenty of wood for everyone.

CHRISTMAS SEASON

When I was a little girl, Christmas wasn't thought about until the first of December. It wasn't commercialized to the degree it is today. That was before the days of the BIG SELL.

Christmas trees were not shipped in from some distant place. We cut our own trees from the surrounding countryside. We couldn't buy the ornate ornaments we can get today. We made most of the items we put on the tree. Japanese paper lanterns, made with tablet paper or of construction paper; paper chains pasted together; strings of popcorn and red haw garlands; paper stars and bells. We got the red haws from trees in the woods and we knew just where they were.

We had no strings of lights. Our only lights were from wax candles that we clipped to the tree's boughs. These were of various colors (not very many). They were lighted for only a short time on Christmas eve. Dad always had a bucket of water and dipper handy in case a flame from a candle might catch the tree afire and burn our house down. This moment of candlelighting was a "Wonder of Wonders" to me when I first witnessed it as a small girl. I can recall the flickering flames of the candles reflecting on the faces of the family as they stood around the tree, and every time I smell cedar or evergreen boughs, I am reminded of that experience.

We didn't get many Christmas presents and perhaps they weren't exactly what we had in mind, but we played with them and were happy.

Colors of red and green are the Christmas colors for me. Evergreen boughs, poinsettias, holly with red berries, red and green paper and ribbons, and baubles and garlands. I'm just an old fashioned girl.

MY VALENTINE BIRTHDAY

I happened to be the first grandchild born into my father's family. He was the oldest son in his family of twelve children, ten of whom lived to maturity. I was born on February 14, Valentines Day, and from that first birthday on, I received a little special attention because of my Valentine birthday.

In the early 1900s the greeting card business had not yet developed to a very great degree. Hallmark Cards hadn't yet been thought of. But there were places where one could get beautiful special cards, like valentines. Some of the postal cards had beautiful scenes printed on them. My dad's younger sisters and Great-Aunt Sue sent me many beautiful valentines through the years. My brother also got some special ones because they didn't want to ignore him. We had a special box where these valentines were kept, and each year we added to the collection. Only on special occasions and times was the box opened and we were allowed to set them up and play with them (some of them were fragile); then they were whisked away after we had enjoyed them for a short time.

I have never seen such elaborate valentines as we had in our collection. I remember several three-dimensional ones. One my brother received was in the shape of a big heart-shaped balloon which had cut-out tissue paper which opened up, much like the paper bells at Christmastime. I treasured one which had an upside down umbrella of pink paper which opened up. They were really works of art.

There was a lot of activity around homes and schools in preparation for exchange of valentines between students. How many people today remember the envelopes of penny valentines? Perhaps ten or twenty in a big envelope? They were often the size of small postcards or heart shaped. We made many of our own valentines; cut red hearts out of construction paper, used crayons and paste. Every room at school had its big valentine box with a big slot for depositing valentines to be given to your friends. Sometimes the box ran over.

Some jokers specialized in sending comic valentines to those they had a dislike for. Sometimes you could get a point across with a comic valentine you couldn't any other way. If you sent a comic one you didn't ever sign it. Those who received them sometimes never did figure out where they came from.

Then, on February 14, the box was opened and the teacher called out the names on them and you went up front and accepted yours. The most popular boy or girl usually received the most valentines, but we all went home that night with a little fist full of valentines. When we got home we knew just how many we had, as we had counted and recounted them.

My Valentine birthday is still a special day to me. The month of February is Birthday Month. I celebrate not only on the 14th, but all month, and get from twenty-five to thirty Valentinebirthday greeting cards. It still makes me feel sort of special.

SPRING HOUSE CLEANING

Before the era of electricity, the housekeeper had only the mop, broom, feather duster and soap and water for tidying up the home. One couldn't dust until the sweeping was done and the dust had settled. Oil mops were used on the bare floors.

Probably, because I was the only girl, I was included in so many household activities and chores. My mother told me: "You may not have to do your own housework when you grow up and have a home of your own, but you will know how it should be done and be able to give directions to someone else." On Saturdays and after school hours, it seemed I was always called on to run errands, "bring this or that," or "go out there and get a needed item," and "bring it here." These times were always multiplied when Spring House Cleaning time came.

We always had to wait until it was warm enough to take down the heating stove and stove pipe and put it away for the summer. The hole in the wall where the pipe came out of had to be cleaned out and the stopper put in. Most of these stoppers were tin with a pretty picture on them. All the bedding was put on the clothesline to air. Mattresses were carried out in the sun and the dust was beaten out of them with carpet beaters. All the spare quilts and blankets were aired and the ones in use were washed and dried.

It seemed like the whole house was torn up. Everything was taken down, pictures off the wall, curtains from the windows. The walls were all wiped down. If the walls were painted, they were someties washed between paintings. Good sized rugs were rolled and taken outside, thrown over the clothesline and beaten to get the dust out. In those days, the only carpet sweeper anybody had was the little "Bissell," which had a rotating brush whose only function was to pick up lightweight material-like lint and small particles of trash off the rug.

Of course, at this time the lace curtains were taken down from the windows and washed; they had to be stretched on frames with rows of tack points, and they sure made your fingers sore. The windows had to be washed, not only at this time, but several times during the year because of the condensation and dust, which made a dirty film on the inside. Spring house cleaning was a horrendous undertaking, but when it was all done everything smelled so fresh and clean. Today, we can have a clean smelling house everyday of the year with controlled temperatures and filtered, moisture-controlled air. The expression "The Good Old Days" doesn't apply to this housekeeping activity.

OUR SWEET APPLE TREE

It was an old tree, when I was born early in the twentieth century, and it stood strong and sturdy, not too far from our back door at the farm home.

We lived on the farm my great-grandfather started as a young man. At his death, my father bought the farm, and my GreatGrandmother Lamer lived out her life with my family on what had been her farm. I can barely remember her, but I have been told that I was her shadow, always there with her. We were "buddies." She had little formal education, but she taught me what she could; how to count, to spell and to read. She trained me so well that I didn't have to go to first grade at all, but entered public school at the second grade level.

This old apple tree which grew in grandma's backyard was no ordinary tree. I am sure that someone set it out with special care, and there aren't any wild apple trees in the woods to transplant. It was a rare one. The apples were never any color but green, even when they were ripe; oh, maybe they had a little yellow tinge. They were the sweetest apples you ever tasted, and the meat was yellow. I do not think we ever cooked the apples, made applesauce or apple pies. I do not know if they were even edible when cooked. We had several acres of apple trees on the farm, but this tree was the only one of its kind.

But it was a beautiful tree, well shaped and always full of blossoms and buzzing bees when in bloom. It was a good backyard tree, providing shade to sit under and to play as a child. The trunk of the tree was very large and the limbs spread out like a giant umbrella. It must have been very strong too, for it had a rope swing with a board seat hanging from one of the large limbs. One of my early memories relating to the tree was having the rope on the swing break with my dad and me in the swing, and we came down with a big crash and I suppose the usual tears, etc. There were no broken bones. I don't remember much about the swing after that spill. "Someone" must have thought it too dangerous, and it just "went away."

Time passed; we continued to grow, and the old sweet apple tree still bloomed every spring and produced a few good apples each year, always sweet. Several neighboring farmers kept bees and the tree was a good source for the nectar they needed to make honey in blooming season each year. I am sure that many birds nested in its branches and sang their songs to us each year, but those memories have gone.

I wasn't the only child growing up in that house on the farm. I had a brother about two years younger than me. We both had red hair, which was unheard of anywhere in our families. Nobody could remember anyone in our families having red hair, except our dear little Great-Grandmother Lamer.

Early one winter afternoon, our mother went upstairs for a nap, and my brother and I were told to be good children and stay out of trouble. I do not remember our ages, but my brother was fascinated with matches about that time. The old apple tree had some hollow places near the ground at the base of the trunk and brother built a little fire in one of those hollows. It was easy to do, with the dry leaves, etc. he found lying around. The fire got out of hand and I wanted to go tell mom what was happening, but he persuaded me not to go, but to stay with him. About this time mom woke up and looked out the window to see smoke coming out of the old tree, all up and down, as there were limbs with hollow places all over the tree making drafts for smoke. She came down and got things under control. We were both punished because I didn't come and tell her sooner. To this day, I am not sure whether the enjoyment of the fire kept me there, or that I let him threaten or intimidate me.

Needless to say, life for the Old Sweet Apple Tree was all downhill from the time of the fire. Parts of it began dying and finally it had to be cut down. When the limbs were sawed in proper lengths and it was stacked, it was ready to provide much of our fuel that winter. No effort was made to replace the apple tree, but we missed the shade and presence of the tree that was our friend for so long, season after season.

TO TOWN ONCE A WEEK

Usually we went to Cobden every Saturday afternoon. I had my piano lesson at that time too. We were also treated to a trip to the ice cream parlor. That was the time for the family to stock up on grocery staples. On the farm, at times, we had several dozen eggs we didn't use, so we took them to the grocery store and got credit on our bill for them. And sometimes, when the cow provided a goodly supply of milk and we made more butter than we could use, we took it to the grocery also, and were paid for it. My mother was known for her good country butter and the grocer had no trouble finding a buyer for it. The grocer men usually gave us "due bills," and I am sure that is where the term "butter and egg" money came from.

We stocked up on staples, buying 100 pound sacks of sugar, and twenty-five pounds of flour, and kerosene by the five-gallon can for our lamps. You might wonder why we bought so much sugar, but we needed it for canning fruits, and making jams and jellies, cakes, candies, etc. There were no sugar substitutes. We had our own lard, milk, butter and vegetables.

This weekly trip to town was probably the only time we were away from home, except to go to school and maybe church on Sunday. For several years we attended the Toledo Christian Church, which was just down the road from our farm house. Uncle Witt Lamer's house was in between. My Sunday school teacher when I started to Sunday school was also my first grade teacher, Mrs. Leta Smith, and I was very fond of her. Later, when we had a car, we went to the Presbyterian Church in Cobden, which was my mother's church.

Towns, or villages the size of Cobden, had two or three general stores where you bought most everything you needed: seeds to plant, yard goods, underwear, bed clothes, shoes, shirts, all kinds of thread and garden tools and most of them had groceries also.

We were fortunate in having the Illinois Central Railroad, which ran north and south through the town. At one time, there were eight passenger trains, four each way, which stopped every day. It was the direct line north to St. Louis and Chicago and south to Cairo,

New Orleans and Miami. Some of the passenger trains did not stop, except on special occasions, or to pick up or discharge some person of importance. In that case, the station operator was instructed to flag the train and it stopped. This was all by special arrangement.

Our stores might have been limited in the variety of merchandise they could supply us with, but we had another source of supply in the mail order catalog. The most used ones were Sears and Roebuck, and Montgomery Ward and Co. One of the best pasttimes we had on rainy days was to study the catalog to learn just what was available and could be wished for and eventually ordered and received through the mail. Of course, there was always the matter of trying to determine what size was needed or how many yards were required. One could never be sure what the color would be that we wanted, as most of the catalogs were printed in black and white. But your order came to the mail box (down by the public road), and the mailman brought it along with the other mail, as we always had rural mail service. Sometimes you had to send some of your order back in exchange for a smaller or larger size or different color. But this was only a matter of time. The postage wasn't very much. Some folks even ordered their shoes from the mail order catalog, but we were never very successful doing that. The mail order catalog was the country folk's way of knowing the styles of the day and the changes in fashion from time to time.

SPECIAL SOCIAL EVENTS

ICE CREAM SOCIALS

When I was growing up, the people in small communities were close to each other and they pooled their resources and talents and planned get-togethers and money-raising affairs for one cause or another.

Ice cream socials were usually planned by churches or women's groups of the church. They were really a social event. Women froze freezers (usually one or two-gallon freezers) of homemade, custard-style ice cream. They also baked cakes and pies and sometimes made sandwiches. This was at a time when we couldn't buy quantities of ice cream at the grocery store. There was usually one ice cream parlor in a small town and the ice cream wasn't the special quality home-cooked and frozen ice cream had. The ice cream was scooped out of the freezer and sold by the dish. Pies were sold by the wedge (usually six pieces to the pie), and cakes by the piece. Five-gallon containers of REAL lemonade were made and sold by the glass.

If there were extra cakes, and sometimes the best cooks prepared special cakes, they were sold at auction to the highest bidder and the auctioneer tried to get extra money for them. These affairs were socials, but they were planned primarily to raise money for the church and usually for some specific purpose that the regular budget didn't take care of.

These ice cream socials were held on the church lawns, in the hot summertime, and were very well attended and supported by neighbors and friends. I can remember going to ice cream socials at the Toledo country church, down the road, when I was a very little girl, and later to the church socials in the town of Cobden.

During World War I, hundreds of dollars were raised for the Red Cross at ice cream socials in the vicinity of Cobden. Most everybody in the community took part. They donated ice cream and cakes and pies and then came and paid for what they ate. They were widely publicized. Children looked forward to an ice cream social. There was a lot of running and playing "on the edges" of the crowd, with many admonitions of "stay out of the way," from the workers at the social.

PIE SUPPERS

Every country school, and occasionally the village school in Cobden, had regular times for pie suppers as money-raising affairs. The women and girls brought home-baked pies in specially decorated boxes. We pasted colored crepe paper on the boxes (chosen to make a pleasing combination of colors, with a design of our own), and also managed to put a bow and frills on the box. Every girl and her mother wanted her to have the prettiest box and the best pie there. I suppose that is what all the decorating was about.

Every pie, or box with the pie in it, was given a number, and the list of numbers and "bringers" of the pies was circulated among the people in attendance, so everyone knew whose pie was being sold. A good auctioneer knew that certain pies would bring top money, because of the popularity of the girls and the interest of the young men present. Running up the price of a pie on a girl's boyfriend was one of the sports of the event. Sometimes a group of boys would pool their resources to keep the girl's steady boyfriend from getting her pie, or at least make him pay a handsome price for it. A good auctioneer could sense these situations and get all the money he could from the auction.

Sometimes the event evolved into a box supper. In that case the pretty box contained the elements of a full meal, like sandwiches or fried chicken, potato salad, pickles, devilled eggs and cookies or cake.

LAST-DAY-OF-SCHOOL PICNICS

In country schools, the "last-day-of-school" picnic was an annual event. It was planned to display some of the classroom work and award prizes for spelling, arithmetic, writing, drawing, attendance, etc. Every family brought a basket full of food and the food was spread on long tables on the lawn, or inside if it was too cool or rainy.

For the scholar, "last-day-of-school" was a very special day. We had them at Cobden Grade School, but they weren't as well attended as the country school affairs. Every girl always had to have a special dress for the occasion. We didn't always have a picnic with food, but the awards were given and our work displayed.

In country schools, the teachers staggered the days of "letting out" at the several schools so that neighboring teachers and scholars could attend their neighbor's picnic and last-day-ofschool activities.

THE CHARIVARI

This was a custom that sometimes followed a marriage, and it was planned to harass and call attention to a newly-married couple (all in good fun). Sometimes it was delayed, if the couple could afford a honeymoon, until they returned home.

Friends and neighbors and members of the families of the bride and groom plotted to stage the charivari at the first opportunity they had to find the bride and groom together, usually at the bride's or groom's parents' home, or in their new home, if they had one. The group of people brought anything that would make a noise: shot guns, pistols, horns, buckets with rocks in them, pans to beat on, anything that would add to the din. They kept up the commotion and noise until the bride and groom made an appearance at the door to invite the intruders in. A treat by the bride and groom was usually expected. Charivaris were planned to embarrass the groom more than the bride. Sometimes the men tried to ride him on a rail or otherwise make him uncomfortable. Charivari crowds were made up of young and old alike.

QUILTING BEES

When I was a little girl, every home had a shelf of homemade quilts. There were various, fancy-patterned, pieced quilts, but the most common was the nine-patch. If you had a quilt, pieced and ready to quilt, you sent out a call for help and all your friends and neighbors came in for the day and helped you quilt it. Every home usually had some quilting frames or you could borrow some. The women invited spent the entire day quilting and visiting and "gossiping" (exchanging news items). The hostess (the woman with the quilt) furnished the lunch and it usually was a sumptuous one. One man, so he told me, learned a lot about life, as a little boy, from sitting quietly and unknown at his mother's feet, under the quilting frames. When the day was over, the quilt was usually done, that is, if it wasn't quilted in a fancy pattern. One of the most common of quilting patterns was the shell.

ORGANIZED ACTIVITIES

CHURCHES

There were four churches in Cobden and numerous little country churches scattered through the surrounding countryside. Later the Baptist church had a faction that split from the First Baptist and became the Emmanuel Baptist Church.

This group of churches included a Catholic Church with quite a sizeable congregation. Most of the members were of German extraction and were probably the only ethnic group in the community and most of them were farmers. Many of them had come to this country to escape service in the German army.

I remember at one time the churches pooled their resources and arranged for an evangelist and song leader to come and hold a revival meeting in a tent, which wasn't very large, but seemed so to me. This tent was put on a vacant lot in the town of Cobden, and for two weeks was filled with people. There was a lot of preaching and enthusiastic singing and some people were converted and many revitalized, or recharged. I was just a little girl, but I remember the excitement it generated.

THE LADIES AID SOCIETY AND BAZAARS

Every church of any size had a Ladies Aid Society, which met for study and planned money-raising functions to help the church in its work. They usually pledged a certain amount toward the church expenses, sometimes earmarked for an improvement in the church building or some decorative item. They planned ice cream suppers or socials, annual fried chicken dinners and bazaars. Sometimes they would cater a special meal for a local organization.

The Ladies Aid passed the presidency around and every member had a chance to be president or leader, for a year. They worked through ways and means committees and other officers. The annual bazaars were usually held in the fall, because most of the summer canning and preserving had been done and the housewives had more time to give. But items to sell were made all during the year. One of the sale items was fancy kitchen aprons, and a quilt was sometimes raffled off (numbers sold and the lucky one drawn from a hat). On the day of the bazaar, a chicken pie dinner was served at noon and we all got to go. The church I attended served suet pudding; I looked forward to enjoying this hot, spicy dessert each bazaar day.

In addition to the Ladies Aid Society, our church had a Missionary Society where women who believed in missions (and some thought all money earned from money-raising projects should stay in the community) met to discuss work going on in the several mission fields, both home and foreign. They donated a set sum per member and also planned and carried out their own moneyraising projects. They were a smaller group than the Ladies Aid.

Then we also had a Junior Ladies Aid made up of younger women, single and married, and that group was quite active, patterning their activities after the older group. Many members stayed on with the Junior Aid, years after they should have joined the senior group. This was probably because they resisted everything that would tend to make them seem older.

SINGING SCHOOLS

At times, young and old alike gathered to learn and practice singing together. Four-part harmony was taught, sometimes using shaped notes. This was usually done under the supervision of a teacher, native or imported. One man lived in our community who was a good singer and could teach, and he organized classes. Then others came from neighboring communities and held instructional classes periodically. This kept voices trained for singing in the church choirs and also for home talent shows.

We also had two teachers of piano who were very different in their instructions and way of playing. They were not the best of friends. Both were maiden ladies and each had their own ways of being different from the common herd. It was my privilege to take lessons from one of them for five years.

DANCING CLASSES

Our parents banded together and enrolled us in a dancing class (ballroom dancing, the one-step, two-step, fox trot and waltz) taught by first one teacher and then another. For a while, a couple came twice a month from another town in the county. They hired a pianist and drummer or saxophonist for music. Some of the older persons who liked to dance attended and they were good partners for the learner to practice with. This gave us an activity that was enjoyed by one and all and we all looked forward to the evening we went to dancing class.

One teacher we had came from Carbondale and he brought his patent leather dancing shoes and changed his shoes behind a screen in one corner of the room. We always had a large upstairs room, in one of two places, that could be cleaned up, with a half-way decent floor. These affairs became social activities and order was maintained; no disorders were allowed, so my parents were not afraid to let my brother and me attend. They knew we would not be exposed to a rowdy, unruly crowd. If anyone came under the influence of alcohol, they were asked to leave and during the evening the town marshall made one or two stops in to see if everything was O.K. Usually, the price charged was fifty cents per person. That is where I learned to dance. My brother Frank learned also and he was a beautiful dancer, quite a "showman".

MEDICINE AND HEALTH CARE

Every small town usually had one or two doctors as a rule, one of them an older man, who had a sort of fatherly attitude toward the children and their families. The other would probably be a newcomer, maybe a native son returned, but more likely a doctor from afar, trying his newly acquired knowledge on a new clientele.

You didn't call the doctor until you really thought you could not handle the ailment alone. There were many home remedies, like "an apple a day," mustard plasters, goose grease, castor oil, kerosene and sugar for croup, etc. My mother had a recipe or formula for oil to put on one's chest, when the cold seemed to be going down into the bronchial tubes and chest. First a concoction of turpentine, camphorated oil, camphor, kerosene, castor oil, lard and something she called sweet oil, was warmed and throughly mixed. Then it was rubbed on your chest and your back, and a flannel cloth saturated with the mixture was tied around your neck, so it laid on your chest all night. It was a miserable feeling to have this treatment, in addition to the rest of your miseries. It was all you could smell, if your nose was not stopped up. Next morning you were usually better, but you had to tolerate the flannel cloth for a day or two, just to be sure. The whole house reeked of mom's liniment for chest colds. I still have the recipe for the lotion in my mother's own handwriting, but have never mixed any of it.

One thing you could be sure of; if you called your doctor, **he would come** to see you. Nothing was said about an office call. He couldn't tell you to go to the hospital, for the closest one was fifteen miles away and only dirt roads to get to it.

We had no vaccines to prevent childhood diseases. Go to any cemetery and see the numerous little graves of children who shouldn't have died. Some of the maladies were summer complaint, typhoid fever, membranous croup (which we now know was diphtheria), etc. It was quite a feat to rear all your children to healthy maturity. Many of the diseases were fatal because the doctors didn't know the causes of them nor how to treat them. Diagnostic procedures in those days were not very sophisticated. I know of one or two instances when a child was put on the kitchen table, when he had pneumonia, and the doctor saved the child's life by using the surgical procedure of making an incision and inserting a tube between two ribs to drain off the fluid in the pleural cavity. It was an extreme procedure, but in the cases I know about the children who were treated are still living today, because the doctor used this drastic life-saving measure.

When I was growing up, a person didn't ever think about a hospital until he was about ready to die. That was a stigma that took a long time to overcome. Maybe hospitals were used more for the dying than they were used to keep people healthy. Today, so many diagnostic procedures require that the patient be hospitalized, that we think nothing of being admitted. Certainly, we are not thinking seriously about leaving this life when we go to a hospital for a day or a few days for examination observation.

I believe that the growth of hospitals and hospital care in this country is one of the most phenomenal of any other area of our society. Most people today have had a hospital experience. Our doctors are better trained. They have access to so many wonderful drugs that have been tested and tried for effectiveness. We know more how to care for our bodies and what we need to do to stay healthy. The emphasis is on staying healthy, instead of letting a malady get a hold on us and we are past restoring to normal health.

HUNTING AND CAMPING

My father was an avid duck hunter. He belonged to Grassy Lake Gun Club, situated on one of the many shallow lakes that are in our county, down close to the Mississippi River. They were on low ground and were connected to the big river. When the water in the Mississippi overflowed its banks, it ran into the lakes and kept them filled most of the time. The lakes were shallow and full of water lilies and a marshy growth, whose seed the ducks liked to eat. The ducks came down from Canada to winter at these spots and they were a hunter's paradise. In my childhood days, there was a generous daily limit of ducks allowed to the hunter by law and they were allowed to kill many more than they needed. Sometimes they came home with dozens of them, but they were not wasted. The ones we couldn't eat, were given to friends and neighbors. All of my mother's pillows were of the finest duck down. She also had a feather bed made of down and feathers from the ducks. In time I learned to clean a wild duck and there were times that I wished I had not learned. All my life I have heard of hunting experiences at Grassy Lake.

The members of Grassy Lake Gun Club were from all over. Most of them were from Union County, but some who had left the area for work or professional reasons lived in Chicago and elsewhere. They all came back each year for a hunt during the season. The club had a crude clubhouse on the bank of the lake, built in an "H" form. The crossbar of the H connected the kitchen and eating space with the sleeping area. The only way of heating and cooking was the BIG fireplace at one end of the kitchen. There also was a long table and benches for eating. The walls of the kitchen were lined with lockers which belonged to several members and these were kept locked. They were kept well stocked, for the hunters spent several days at a time hunting on the lake.

The rest of the clubhouse was used for sleeping purposes and bunk beds were lowered from the side walls, where they were kept hooked when not in use. There was a big heating stove in the back room (parallel to the kitchen) to make that part of the house bearably warm. The clubhouse had a front porch where there were buckets and wash pans and soap to "wash up" after a day's hunt. Outside the clubhouse were big boxes of wooden decoys which were always under lock and key. The decoys were beautifully made and were weighted to float on the water properly, and I am sure they were expensive. They were not toys, but as children we thought they were and didn't miss an opportunity to get our hands on one of them.

In the early days, our dads drove a team and a light wagon about fifteen miles down to Grassy Lake for a hunt, so they stayed long enough to make the trip worthwhile. They had a barn where the teams and wagons were kept and a house where the caretaker lived. He looked after the property and clubhouse while they were away. He also farmed some of the tillable land that belonged to the tract they owned.

The families of the Grassy Lake Gun Club members from Cobden were allowed one outing a year at the lake. My, what preparations! We cooked for days. Pies and cakes and gingerbread and sugar cookies. Of course, we always had a duck dinner while we were down there, cooked in the fireplace in dutch ovens. My mother was always assigned the task of making the biscuits (in a big dutch oven) for everyone's breakfast each day. She made three or four big batches and she was a professional. I have never eaten such delicious biscuits. Maybe they were always better when we had to wait for the last batch to bake. With sorghum molasses and fresh country butter they were a delight.

The children in the families ranged in age from six to eighteen. Some of the boys were old enough to go hunting with their dads, but they were few in number. There wasn't much for younger children to do, but we played cards, guessing games and charades and had make-believe shows. The grown-ups played poker and rummy and pinochle. I remember getting up early and dressing before the open fire and going outside before the mists had risen from the water. There was a beautiful haze over everything and it was so different from the morning in the hills north of Cobden.

CAMPING SAFARIS

Because of a holdover from our experiences at Grassy Lake and partly because of the pioneer spirit in our blood, we began to think about going camping in the fall, after the days began to get cool. Some families had large tents for sleeping and a special tent to be used as a mess tent and a place to have shelter in case of rain. Some groups had bedsprings and mattresses they took along. In the group there were always enough iron cooking pots and skillets for cooking over an open fire.

The camp was usually set up on the bank of the Mississippi River, where we could see the riverboats pass by during the day. They would play their seachlights on the camp when they came around the bend at night, not sure just what they were seeing, as the light from the campfire came into their view. We brought precooked food with us and other food was cooked over an open fire, on the site. We slept on straw and washed in river water, taking milk cans of drinking water with us. It was fun to play at being adventurers (well, modified ones) for a few days. Sometimes when it rained while we were in camp, we really learned what roughing it could mean. It was always good to get back to our own beds, the shelter of our homes and the luxury of a good hot bath.

MEMORIAL DAY MAY 30

The first Memorial Day in the U.S.A. was initiated by General John A. Logan of Murphysboro, Illinois to honor the Union soldiers who gave their lives to the Union in the Civil War. At that time, there were many living veterans who had fought for the Union in the war between the states. The ex-soldiers called themselves the Grand Army of the Republic. In 1926, sixty-one years after the Civil War, in the little community of Cobden, there were eleven veterans of that conflict receiving pensions. For years after W.W.I, the American Legion kept this special day alive, a day of honor to our war dead.

On Memorial (Decoration) Day, all the countryside cemeteries in the county, where the veterans were buried, were visited. Their graves were newly marked by crosses and American flags and a short graveside service given in their memory, complete with taps by members of the American Legion. The legion also arranged for a special community church service (with churches rotating) for the Sunday morning nearest Memorial Day, in memory of meritorious service given by our men in uniform for our country.

Every little town had a patriotic parade with bands and bugle corps, and cars and bicycles decorated with red, white and blue. Perhaps there might be a few floats. There were patriotic speeches emphasizing heroism and patriotism in defense of our country. Band concerts were sometimes given. It was all planned to gather people together to hear and to think about our history and our country, and the role of the citizen and soldier in keeping us free.

Today, Memorial Day has evolved into a home-coming activity in many communities. The soldiers' graves still have their crossed flags. Families meet and renew acquaintances. We decorate everybody's graves, not just the soldiers. Since civil war days we have had several wars and conflicts, including two world wars and our Korean and Vietnam conflicts, which we wish we could forget.

As a little girl, I remember my activities on Memorial Day. It seemed that my mother had more ancestors buried in our little Cobden cemetery than anyone else. Her mother and father and both sets of her grandparents were interred there. My father's people were also there. Besides, there were dear friends who also had to be remembered. For days we combed the countryside for blooming wild flowers, field daisies, ferns of all descriptions, yarrow (a meadow flower) and wild roses. Sometimes we had to resort to little sprigs of honeysuckle. Even when I was real small, I went along with mom as she decorated the graves. Those were some of the "step and fetch it" days. There was always water to carry, etc. Sometimes we were commanded, "Come over here, that is a grave you are standing on."

TRIPS TO THE DEEP WOODS

We always walked on our trips to the woods at the north end of our farm. The walks were usually taken in the late spring or early summer, before the weather was too hot. One feature of the pasture we had to cross first, was the rail fence where the wild blackberries and wild roses bloomed. There were always some strands of barbed wire strung along the fence and we were lucky to get over the fence without snagging a hole in something. There were about a dozen hickory nut (scaly bark) trees in the pasture. Several cows were always grazing there, but they were always gentle.

We had to walk down and down in the deep woods to get to the spring. The ground was covered with years and years of fallen dead leaves. New plants came up each year through the leaves. I haven't forgotten how cool and fresh the water from the spring tasted when we drank from the leaf cup mom made for us. Neither have I forgotten the fresh, green, cool smell all around. There were always seasonal wild flowers to pick, but we had to watch and be careful not to touch the poison ivy, which was there too. The banks were covered with fern. Maidenhair fern was always so dainty and graceful with its shiny black stems. You will only find it in deeply shaded woods.

When we were small, this was a long trek, but when we grew older we went further and would swing on the wild grapevines hanging down from the trees, making fine rope-like swings like Tarzan used.

INDEPENDENCE DAY - JULY 4TH

In the early 1900s, every county had a 4th of July celebration at the county fairgrounds. We all knew that this was in celebration of gaining our freedom as a colony from Great Britain. We grew up very proud of our free country and revered and honored those who fought in the Revolutionary War in order for us to be free.

Most of the children didn't get to the county seat for the big 4th of July celebration where they had races and all the attractions that go with a big fair. There was always a balloon ascension. I can remember seeing the gas filling the balloon all day, the cloth of the balloon weaving back and forth. When the balloon was released later in the day, we could see it in the sky from our home, seven miles away.

We had picnics in our little villages and family get-togethers. There was patriotic speaking, bands, and parades, always ending with fireworks paid for by merchants and outstanding citizens.

At home we always had homemade ice cream and our own private fireworks which lighted up the front lawn. We were allowed sparklers and little Chinese firecrackers, which we stuck in a spool on a stick and were allowed to hold in our hand, always being reminded not to get them too close to our eyes. We were allowed to hold small Roman candles, but the rockets had to be carefully placed on a board and fired by an adult. We were careful not to have accidents.

Years and years later, after my first experiences with 4th of July celebrations, I was privileged to see the musical 1776, a play based on the signing of the Declaration of Independence, and I had a still deeper feeling of what the 4th of July really means to us. The play showed how the people who wrote the declaration met in Philadelphia in the hot summertime and worked out the wording of that document. Everytime we think of the Declaration of Independence, we should be grateful to these dedicated men who had the vision of freedom from oppression, as well as to those who fought and died for that freedom.

CHILDREN SELDOM GOT BORED

In the years of my growing up, children didn't expect or demand to be entertained and they were rarely bored with life. We had plenty of chores to do daily and after they were done, we created our own entertainment. There were many games, handed down from generation to generation: games like LEAP FROG, TAG, HOP-SCOTCH, HIDE AND SEEK, BLIND MAN'S BLUFF and ANDY OVER. The latter was played with a homemade ball of string which we threw back and forth over a low-roofed building, with some of us on one side of the building and the rest of us on the other. The ball didn't quite get across sometimes and rolled back in the gutter, so a ladder had to be kept handy to get it out. Most all our games involved activity of some sort, but of course inside games had to be resorted to when the weather was bad.

In those days, most every boy had a sack of marbles. Sometimes they let the girls play, particularly the tomboys, like me. They played marbles more in the spring. The games required a clean, hard-surfaced place to outline the oval that was used to position the marbles. You were fortunate if you had a rug inside the house that had a pattern you could use as a marble court. The game of marbles was very hard on knees of stockings and overalls. You weren't supposed to play for "keeps" but most everyone did at times.

There were no radios in our homes. Most of the news we got was from a day-late newspaper from St. Louis or Chicago. A few families had Victrolas and when we went to visit, they would play the few records they had, like; "The Stars and Stripes," a march by J. Philip Sousa; "The Whistler and his Dog;" or Caruso's "Oh, Sole Mio." Most communities had an auditorium or opera house where travelling lyceum shows performed several times a year. There were also travelling tent shows which came around several times a year, usually in the summer. We used to know some of the people who were with these shows. More amateurish were some of the home talent shows and colored minstrels which our community staged periodically. All of these forms of entertainment were "corny" as compared to the

sophisticated entertainment our children see today on
the TV screens in their own homes. They are exposed
to the same talent seen on Broadway and on the stage
at Las Vegas.

When a child has entertainment ready-made most
of his waking hours, it is probably the normal thing
to be bored when on a vacation trip away from the
"boob tube."

SOUNDS AND SMELLS

There are a few things I recall about growing up on a farm that I haven't been able to include in any of my stories, so I have to write about them separately. To some, these qualities of life would go unnoticed and be considered unimportant, but to me some of the things I heard and the scents that I smelled made a lasting impression on me. Children who grow up in cities never experience the sounds and smells I will try to describe as I remember them.

Many of the sounds could be heard at dusk or in the early morning hours. The times that I remember them were when other noises where hushed, and it was easier to hear them. I remember the little frogs and the big ones too, who began their chorus from the ponds and marshes early spring evenings when our windows were open. Then, at the same time, tree frogs and dry flies and cicadas contributed their parts to the symphony from the trees. This was the music that lulled me to sleep many nights. One of my bedroom windows looked out on a pasture where there was a shallow pond and there were trees in the yard outside my other window.

If you lived near a wooded area, the whip-poor-will's repetitive call (whip-poor-will, whip-poor-will), could be identified over the hills and valleys in the early evening and sometimes most of the night. If they came close to the house, the drumming sound became offensive and could prevent restful sleeping. Occasionally, in the the country at night, one of the many species of owls can be heard. One of the most common owls is the little screech owl, whose eerie call sounds like some one in distress.

Do you remember hearing a rooster crow at "first light?" How long has it been since you heard that sound? Maybe you are not familiar with it. But that is a sound very common to those who live in the country and start the day's work at an early hour in the morning.

One of the daytime sounds is the one that the purple martins make as they busily come and go from the house you have provided for them on a pole in the farm yard. They like to be near people. They never touch the ground, getting all their food in the air and they like to perch on telephone wires and roof tops.

Another daytime bird that can easily be identified by its call is the quail or bobwhite. Its call sounds like "bob white," hence its common name. These birds like cover and they are difficult to see because of their markings; but if one calls, it usually gets an answer from another bird, sometimes quite a distance away.

Have you ever seen a mother hen with a flock of chicks? I remember hearing her "clucking" to her brood, scratching around on the ground and in the grass to uncover insects for her young ones to eat. Then I remember at times she would stop and cock her head to one side and make a "buzzing" sound. This was a warning to her chicks to run for cover, for she thought there might be a chicken hawk somewhere close. If there was a hawk near, the purple martins would swoop down and chase it away. That was one reason to have the birds live in a colony in the yard.

Smells, I know, will be a little harder to describe, but they are distinctive memories just the same. One smell is that of new-mown hay, particularly when it is being turned and raked. Or, the smell of the first few raindrops in a dusty road at the beginning of a summer shower. This is one smell I remember vividly. I think that city people have a different feeling about rain than the people in the country. Rain in the city is a nuisance only, but to country people it is very necessary for growing crops and very welcome when it comes. I know it rains on city streets and alleys, but nothing on earth smells like rain in a dusty lane in the country.

In some places on country roads, the banks on each side of the road are covered with honeysuckle vines. The smell of these blossoms is delightful in the early evening. You can appreciate it more if you walk down the road or ride slowly in a convertible automobile. If you could find a horse and buggy, it would be fine too.

If you have ever shucked corn or shelled corn by hand, you can remember how the corn crib smelled. This smell also brings to mind the barn and farm animals and the hay loft where feed for the animals was stored.

I can never forget the smells that came from a country kitchen. The tantalizing smell of homemade light bread just out of the oven is one that can come from any kitchen, but I think it smelled better when it came

out, deliciously brown and crusty, from the oven of a wood-burning range in the country. There were also days when the air reeked with pickling spices, when the kettles of hot cucumbers were about ready for canning.

One of the homiest smells is that of smoke from a wood-burning fireplace, as it wafts its way toward the ground on the outside of a home. When I was growing up, we didn't have a fireplace, but we burned wood in stoves for cooking and heating and there was plenty of wood smoke.

These are all nostalgic memories (just a few) I have, that bring to mind a flood of early experiences I had as a girl on the farm.

IMMEDIATE FAMILY PERSONALITIES

Our son, Kirby, thought this little book would not be complete unless it contained some description of the persons in our home as I remembered them. He grew up in the home with his grandparents and treasures that relationship and he wanted his children to know something about their personalities. So, I'll try to paint some word pictures of them.

My mother was a woman of strong convictions and high standards. Her father was the oldest son of a pioneer family in the county, and alcohol ruined his life and kept him from accumulating anything for his hard work. He was a farmer and a good gunsmith, so I have been told. Mom could trace her ancestry back to revolutionary war time and at one time both of us were members of the Daughters of the American Revolution, but we dropped our membership. She was very proud, but did not think of herself as being better than others. She was super sensitive of what her friends and neighbors thought of her and her family. One of her admonitions was, "don't let them see you doing anything that would cast suspicion on you." She was very talented and innovative in an artistic way. She taught me how to draw and do water colors. I was eager to learn and healthy and strong, so I learned how to do many things that other girls were never taught. She always told me, "you may not have to do all the cleaning jobs that go on around a house, but you will know how they ought to be done, and you can more ably supervise." She was a very outgoing woman and had a diffucult time with me, for I was very bashful and shy. I expected others to make the first, friendly move. But I had a big, friendly smile and that helped. But at times I seemed to be tongue-tied.

My father was the oldest of eleven of a family of German descent. He also was a person of high standards and was very honest and very even tempered. Mom was quick tempered, but got over it very fast. Dad learned that if they were to get along as man and wife, he had to learn to not take offense or pout after her outbusts of temper, but just ignore her. If he had an unpleasant task to do, like having to settle a difference with someone who had wronged him, he would not act until he had carefully thought it out and could go about it in a calm, deliberate way. He usually got his point across. Dad only had an 8th-grade education because he had to start manual labor early in life, to help his father support his big family. His father was a carpenter and my mother said dad was a good "barn carpenter." He wasn't a cabinetmaker by any means.

I can remember that mom and dad always agreed on discipline. We could never work one against the other. They were both twenty-five years old when they married and it was five years before I came along. Then in less than two years, I had a little red-headed brother. You might say they had two babies at the same time. Frank (or Red), my only brother, was very ill when he was less than two years old and they almost lost him. As a result, he grew up pampered and protected. He knew that he could get by with some of his shenanigans. As a result, he escaped being reprimanded when he teased me and he used that teasing to "get my goat," so to speak. He made my life miserable at times, for he was a cruel tease. I didn't understand when I was young why he had to be so mean, but after I grew up I could see he only teased those he cared for; he didn't bother those he had no use for. But I still think it was a very ineffective way to demonstrate affection. It wasn't very convincing.

PROGRESS AND CHANGE

I mentioned in another part of this book that in our home we always had a telephone, the wall type, with a crank. It rang constantly (it seemed at times), to service about thirteen homes along a fairly central route that extended about three miles north of the village of Cobden. Nowadays it would be called a small cooperative venture. The owners of the telephones built the line and were responsible for keeping them repaired. I can remember the rapport that went on when something happened to break the line, like a sleet storm or a severe windstorm blowing and breaking tree limbs, which fell onto the lines and broke them.

Our part of the county was a little more progressive than most. A family in Cobden started a small electric plant, generating electric current themselves, for the use of people in the village. Our group of farmers, north of town, organized and helped to build their own electric line, just as they had the telephone, only they had to buy their electricity, by having meters installed and paying for the current they used. This was done about 1916, when I was in the 5th grade. It was wonderful to reach up and turn on the bulb, which hung by a drop cord in the middle of every room, and have the entire room lighted up, even in the corners. We did not have fancy light fixtures and there were no wall switches. We had lots of power failures, for one reason or another and the service wasn't the best in the world, but it was better than kerosene lamps. Later, the electric company was sold to Central Illinois Public Service Co. Then of course our rates went up, but we got better service.

The coming of electricity also changed some other areas of our country living. We could have some electric appliances, like electric fans, vacuum cleaners and toasters, and my father somehow devised an electric motor which ran a washing machine by pulleys (machine attached to a wooden bench). This contraption also had a wringer which moved down the bench to take the clothes from one tub to another without the benefit of a hand-turned crank. This was a wonderful help. But I recall it was difficult to keep in working order and refused to work at the most inopportune times.

In 1917, we had our first automobile, a secondhand Model T touring car, with isinglass curtains in case of rain or wind. You could never get them up after the rain started without getting wet. So if it looked like rain you put them on in advance, to be ready. A few people in the town of Cobden had automobiles several years before we did, but these families were either moneyed ones or those that had a mechanical flair for keeping their machines running. These cars required lots of attention and were used mostly for pleasure, like Sunday afternoon drives. They were seldom driven after dark, for they had gas headlights which gave a very dim light. They had to be hand cranked and were sometimes hard to start. At times, on a cold morning, hot water had to be poured on something you called "the manifold," and then you had to keep the engine running so it wouldn't quit on you. Spark plugs became coated with carbon very frequently and had to be cleaned and something called the magneto had to have the points filed. The tires were very vulnerable to any sharp object in the road and would lose air and become flat very often. A tire pump was part of the equipment of every automobile, along with a box of tire patch for the inner tube which held the air.

But from the time we had our first second-hand automobile, we always had one to get around in; we didn't have to rely on a horse and buggy. Of course, in a few years our second-hand car was pretty shabby and we got a brand new black Model T touring car (still with the isinglass curtains, and having to be cranked). This is the first car I learned to drive, about 1925. Then, in 1926, dad bought our first enclosed car, a Model A sedan, which was somewhat special. I think it must have been "one of a kind." I never heard of another. It had a special gear shift and a special axle which gave it more power to climb a hill or get out of a mud hole.

We had an automobile to take us here and there for pleasure and also for errands, but as long as my father owned his own farm, he used horses and mules to work the farm. He never owned a tractor.

We had better roads "out our way" than most communities, because periodically money was collected for grading and putting lime rock on the roadbed. The road taxes that were levied by district and by the county were so small that they would do little more than pay for grading the dirt roads and filling the mud holes on county roads. The first gravel roads in Union County that were built more than a mile from the towns they entered, were gravelled by private donations. When a mudhole developed on our three-mile stretch of road, the people who lived along the road immediately got the money to pay for extra limestone or rock gravel to repair it. They saw to it that the road was fit to travel the year around. I can remember my folks discussing the matter of road repair, naming those who had given willingly and whose who refused, but traveled the same roads to town.

In 1922, the state of Illinois began to pave the road in front of our home. It was originally State Route 2, and later became U.S. 51. We called the paved road the "hard road," which was a colloquialism common to southern Illinois. This Route 2 started at the Wisconsin line and ran to Cairo, Illinois. Like the Illinois Central Railroad, from Carbondale to Dongola, it had more curves and hills than any other thoroughfare in the state. In 1922, it was said, or so the story goes, that no contractor would take the contract on this section of the road from Carbondale to Cobden, because they feared the concrete would run down the hills before it hardened. So that section of Route 2 was built by the Illinois State Highway Department, which brought a lot of young engineers and road experts into our little town and this caused quite a flurry among the single women, both young and old.

It took many years to procure the right-of-way for U.S. 51, because every influential farmer (and there were many of them) wanted the new highway to be built right in front of his home. They used their influence as individuals and organizations to try to influence and sway the minds of politicians and others to get this done. This is one of the reasons that old route U.S. 51 is so crooked. Another reason is that these roads were built before the days of large earth-moving equipment, and every cubic foot of dirt was moved by horsepower, slip scrapers and Fresno scrapers (which were large slip scrapers between two wheels, pulled by four horses). The building of this

76

road provided road work for local residents along the way and some of the most efficient teamsters from our little town followed this highway building activity to other parts of the state, even as far north as Effingham, Illinois. The crooked, hard road that was built or started in 1922, now has been replaced by Interstate 57, which is a much straighter highway.

My father sold the farm in 1920 to the American Fruit Growers Inc. of Pittsburg, Pennsylvania, but continued working for them as farm manager unitl 1925. He bought a large lot in Cobden, tore down an old house and built a new two-story bungalow-type house. We moved to the village of Cobden in 1926 and life on the farm was over for me.

WOULD I GO BACK?

The answer is definitly NO, if you mean would I like to live under conditions as they were in the early 1900s. I like to think back over some of the experiences I had as a little girl in the country. Life had a quality of simplicity which we do not have today. We were contained in one little corner of the world. We didn't know what was happening in Iran or El Salvador or Russia or China; things that disturb us so much today. The news media somehow tend to make us think we (our nation) are to blame indirectly for all the troubled spots in the world. We are bombarded by newspapers and TV.

We have made so many advances in our culture and knowledge in scientific fields. We are better informed, but we haven't learned any better how to get along with our friends and neighbors. Human nature is pretty much the same as it has always been. But when I stop to consider it, I am amazed at how much our environment has changed since I was a little girl.

It would be difficult to go back to burning wood for heat; to washing clothes on a tin wash board; to walking most everywhere we go; and I am grateful that our surroundings and our advances contribute so much to our comfort. I can really appreciate and I am grateful for the conveniences of modern living.

So, I am willing to give up the simple, sometimes relaxed kind of living, for something much more comfortable—but complicated.